THE NEWS
and other poems

THE NEWS

and other poems

DAVID CITINO

University of Notre Dame Press   Notre Dame, Indiana

Copyright © 2002
University of Notre Dame
Notre Dame, Indiana 46556
All Rights Reserved
http://www.undpress.nd.edu

Library of Congress Cataloging-in-Publication Data
Citino, David, 1947–
The news and other poems / David Citino.
p. cm.
ISBN 0-268-03657-8
ISBN 978-0-268-03658-4 (pbk.)
I. Title.

PS3553.I86 N49   2002
811'.54—dc21
                              2002011997

for
MARY

Contents

Part One. Diggers Unearth Tut's Nurse

Neanderthal, with Help from Cave and Bear, Invents the Flute	5
Diggers Unearth Tut's Nurse	6
Unknown Soldier Buried at Gettysburg	7
Ode to Billie Dove	9
Winnie Ruth Judd, Trunk Murderess	11
The Politics of Biogeography; or, Gerry Adams Visits No. 10 Downing Street	13
Four Drown in Pool	14
Newborn Found Alive in Shallow Grave	16
Models Auction Their Eggs on the Web	18
88-Year-Old Man Visits the Candy Shop	20
Gunman Destroys the World Again	22
25 Hurt in Tent Collapse	24

Part Two. Pompeii in Danger

"I See a Dark Stranger in Your Future"	27
Pompeii in Danger	28
The Road beneath the Road	30
The Farm beneath the Farm	32
Parish Priest Struck by Easter Bell	33
Venice Declares War on Pigeons	34
Funding the Dead	36

Writing to the Holy Child of Aracoeli	38
The Land of Liars	39
Il Giorno to Close	40
Doctors in Italy Transplant Heart of Baby Born without a Brain	41
Nonna, Who, the Last 50 Years, Burned a Candle Every Day	43
Virgin Cries Tears of Olive Oil	44
The Death of Domenico Modugno	46

Part Three. The Penmanship of the Dead

Thoreau's Site Fouled by Nature	49
Making Time	50
The Death of a Friend Who Still Believes	51
The Desertion of the Frogs	53
Tools	55
Payday	57
Naming a Wildflower, a Mountain, a Night	59
Nomen Est Omen: A Name Is Destiny	61
Hound Dog	63
Spiders, Worms, the History of MS	64
Two Lessons from the Sky	65
Reading the MRI Report, the Retired Pastor Considers Dementia	66
Tabloid Poem	69
The Thawing of the Iceman	70
A Brief History of Fathers	72
Calling Mother	73
Song of the Bone	75
The Penmanship of the Dead	76
Sister Mary Appassionata on the Grand Unified Theory	78
Cell Phone	80

Acknowledgments

The author wishes to thank the editors and readers of the following periodicals and anthologies, in which these poems first appeared.

American Literary Review: "Neanderthal, with Help from Cave and Bear, Invents the Flute"

Calapooya: "Tabloid Poem"

The Centennial Review: "Gunman Destroys the World Again," "*Nomen Est Omen:* A Name Is Destiny," "25 Hurt in Tent Collapse"

Chelsea: "Tools"

Cider Press Review: "The Road beneath the Road"

Cortland Review: "Naming a Wildflower, a Mountain, a Night," "Venice Declares War on Pigeons," "Reading the MRI, the Retired Pastor Considers Dementia"

Crab Orchard Review: "The Farm beneath the Farm"

Defined Providence: "Diggers Unearth Tut's Nurse"

Denver Quarterly: "Song of the Bone"

The Georgia Review: "Sister Mary Appassionata on the Grand Unified Theory"

The Hollins Critic: "The Penmanship of the Dead"

The Idaho Review: "88-Year-Old Man Visits the Candy Shop," "The Desertion of the Frogs," "Winnie Ruth Judd, Trunk Murderess," "Calling Mother"

The Literary Review: "Making Time"

Mid-American Review: "Models Auction Their Eggs on the Web"

National Forum: "The Meeting"

New Letters: "Nonna, Who, the Last 50 Years, Burned a Candle Every Day," "Parish Priest Struck by Easter Bell," "Payday"

Ohioana Quarterly: "Cell Phone"

Oxford Magazine: "Pompeii in Danger," "The Politics of Biogeography"

Prairie Schooner: "Unknown Soldier Buried at Gettysburg"

The Prose Poem: "The Land of Liars"

Quarter After Eight: "Hound Dog," "Writing to the Holy Child of Aracoeli"

River City: "The Death of a Friend Who Still Believes"

Salmagundi: "Funding the Dead"

Seneca Review: "Spiders, Worms, the History of MS"

The Southern Review: "Two Lessons from the Sky," "A Brief History of Fathers"

VIA: Voices in Italian Americana: "I See a Dark Stranger in Your Future," "*Il Giorno* to Close"

West Branch: "Virgin Cries Tears of Olive Oil"

Willow Springs: "Four Drown in Pool"

Wind: "Doctors in Italy Transplant Heart of Baby Born without a Brain," "Thoreau's Site Fouled by Nature"

"Newborn Found Alive in Shallow Grave" appears also in *Like Thunder: Poets Respond to Violence in America* (ed. Virgil Suarez and Ryan G. Van Cleave), University of Iowa Press, 2002.

"Ode to Billie Dove" appears also in *And What Rough Beast: Poems at the End of the Century* (ed. Robert McGovern and Stephen Haven), Ashland Poetry Press, 1999.

THE NEWS
and other poems

PART ONE

Diggers Unearth Tut's Nurse

Neanderthal, with Help from Cave and Bear, Invents the Flute

In the dark cave of Slovenia,
    40,000 years of utter silence.
No one to lift this leg bone of bear.

Two finger-holes punched through
    to take the mortal breath away,
end open to let out the skein

of tones closer to human moan
    than human moan, hoot of moon
wind-honed, horned, fervid scents,

fevered puddles of bison blood, beak
    and breath of Gray Father, steam
of Mother Milk. We didn't know

Neanderthals had an ear.
    We didn't know they beatified
their dead with color. In petal,

pistil, stamen they invented
    prayer, and on the first flute
the closer-to-beastly unkin of us

worked, out of starless dark,
    the melodies of bear, and birds
lifting off at dawn. The cave

is a flute, the skull is a flute
    for wish to move through, true,
eye and nose hole waiting for

the skill to finger out our voices.
    From the bones of our parents
we tease out the music of us.

Diggers Unearth Tut's Nurse

From the dry stone of 1330 B.C.
in Saqqara, necropolis near Cairo,

hieroglyphs and the painted figure
of a woman, breast and nipple

exposed, identify Maya, wet-nurse
of Tutankhamun, "Woman

who fed the body of a god."
An honor, this intersection, boy-

god's lips sealed over human nipple,
engorged. All through history

we've forced women to annunciation,
taking from them something closer

to earth to adore, but here's real miracle.
She put to her breast a boy already

shriveling, sickly, tried to chase
away the utter cold of centuries,

milk of her own brief life still
keeping alive the dying god in us.

Unknown Soldier Buried at Gettysburg

The luckiest of all the dead,
he was found where
the fighting began, after
only the first moments of hell.

The archaeologist surmised
he went down hard,
was buried where he fell,
the fat hole in his forehead,

stuck in a shallow grave
and covered quickly—
for there were other skulls
to be cracked, limbs to be

sawed, moans to be lifted
to circle the battlefield
like slow laboring crows.
He was unmarked for 133 years.

The Right Reverend said *We
do not know whether he wore
blue or gray, but we do know
that he bled bright red.*

The Princeton historian
said that the end of the war
meant healing, *So it is
altogether fitting that he sleep*

forever under the flag
of all these United States.
The nonagenarian widows
of a Rebel and a Union soldier

each placed on the casket
a rose, one at the head
and the other at his feet,
because all lives have

the grim, thorny symmetry
of war, two sides, one
marching stronger at the end,
torching fields, the fallen

left behind, below, safe
in a place where crows,
sharpshooters and a brass band
no longer can do them harm.

Ode to Billie Dove

"One of the most beautiful stars of silent film"
—*The New York Times*

And now she's become one
of the most silent stars of film.
She was 97, lived in
the retirement community
of the Motion Picture and Television Fund

with hundreds of others trying
to recall their marks, their cues.
Damsel in distress, her specialty.
Through reels and reels,
Black Pirate, Night Watch, Stolen Bride,

she'd roll her eyes and feign fear
enough to rouse the beast
in every manly breast, so that,
if thoughts could be heard—as
sometimes they are on stage—

theaters would resound with vows,
I'll save you, Billie Dove!
Quaint, this may seem now,
but how hurtful it has always been,
millennia of the fear, coyness, guile

a woman is forced to practice
to make her way with men.
Scenes produced, directed by him.
Still today it sells big time—
the cellar sound she must investigate,

the chase through woods in heels,
or, with moon-pale décolletage,
up from bed to remove the crucifix,
open the window to the squeak,
the flap of undying thirst.

O Billie, you've no need to put
yourself in harm's way now.
You've earned equal billing
with the male lead, a part as large.
Roles are no better today

than seventy years ago, but
now, forever above you
on the door shining bright
as polished marble, a sign
pointing to that far fairer place—

we hope—you have your star.

Winnie Ruth Judd, Trunk Murderess

A longtime friend . . . said that Mrs. Judd had no immediate survivors.
—*New York Times*

A porter spied a pair of fine gams, high heels,
seamed hose, then the dark ooze, pooling
from valise and trunk. He reached down,

put finger to lips, ran like hell to call the cops,
while she made her slinky 25-carat getaway,
a dark lady stepping into the headlights of America.

Eleanor Roosevelt, Melvin Belli, hundreds of pols
and clergy wrote to save her pretty neck from the noose.
Talk about your Damsel in Distress. Crazy

as a siren, they said, but man, those legs, that rack.
And she could cut like a hog butcher or a dago.
Her landlord sold tickets, dime a head, for tours

of the house where two women were shot
in the face as they slept, neatly packaged—
white meat sliced from bone—into history,

while Winnie escaped from the nut house
again and again, headlines like dandelions
rioting up and down the neat lawns.

We've no royal family here, except for
boys and girls who fall for Jezebels and heels
or headlong down wells, kids abused, those who use.

Here, any mother's child can rise or fall.
We kiss those with the dirtiest, softest hands,
especially when they're lovely beyond

our dreams, slipping into the bedroom
to lift the gun to our heads as we breathe,
dream, oblivious—especially if they get off.

The Politics of Biogeography; or, Gerry Adams Visits No. 10 Downing Street

So many
        of
the
    birds
found
      in
    Britain
              are
missing
      from
              Ireland.

Four Drown in Pool

No mass baptism, though we're
deep in the South. This
was truly a total immersion.
From the beginning of time—
before, even—God knew

that the boy who dropped
the ball into the lethal end,
the older boy who tried
to save the bobbing ball
and thrashing boy,

and, one after another,
the two frantic adults,
gasping even before they jumped,
who hadn't time enough
to remove their shoes,

would lose the bubbly struggle
with bleachy water, slip
back into the element
from which it all began.
Now four bodies float face

down, like worshipers
prostrate in the sanctuary,
as submissive as mortals can be.
It makes God sad, because
He's powerless to do

a damn thing about it, fate
and free will being
the rising water table beneath
the pilings and foundation
of the covenant, thunder

stumbling above, or maybe
He has the power but
of His own free will chooses
not to use it, still angry about
bad fruit and snake,

and especially, fig leaves,
the fact that these days
few call His name at all
until something like this
hits close to home

or makes the major media.
It wasn't like these four
were going to live forever,
after all. What is He,
Lifeguard of the Universe?

Everyone has a choice
to learn not to sink. You've
no idea how difficult it is
to be ever above, the one
on whose watch it all happens.

Newborn Found Alive
in Shallow Grave

After that first birth
    out of the soothe of dark,
I was a groan, a bruise, eyes

clenched like fists against the light.
    Having been abused down a tunnel
tight enough to flatten a head,

narrowest way in the world,
    fontanel ticking out my panic,
I was handled harshly

in the mother country, land
    of the loud, unsterile, dry.
I noticed I was naked, heard

the sob and gasp of shame
    that canceled out her childhood.
Out of her mind with me,

she rushed to put me back
    in the dark where only she
could feel my furtive song,

the dirge of one tiny heart.
    I hear the rooting and snort
of the frenzied dogs of evening,

human feet padding behind.
    Once again the mortal dance,
panting struggle upward.

I drag the wet scarlet cord
    no longer tethering this body
to ever. Such howling.

I move to touch the rising moon.

Models Auction Their Eggs on the Web

I praise the holy eggs of models.
    The luscious fallopian tubes down which
jumbo pearls tumble monthly. Also

(Christ, have you seen them?) their legs,
    long as the road leading to paradise
you find in Renaissance paintings

in the best museums, skin smooth
    as the machine-buffed mall floors
and stained glass ceilings

of the finest neighborhoods
    of heaven. I praise the hairs
scented, fine as spun gold

they've plucked, shaved, tweezed,
    dipilitated and air-brushed
so their French-cut panties,

the (Whoa, praise God!) thongs
    fit them like the stupefied gaze
of the world, give them the shape

of the fourteen-year-old girl
    who's just begun to suffer the loss
of perfect eggs of her own. I praise

the tint, the puffy thrust of collagen lips.
    O those scarlet toenails peeking out,
the three-inch heels. O, yes,

the sacred promise of those eggs,
    the allure, the weak-kneed ache
in the crotch of utter beauty, holy

holy Jesus Christ Our Lord Amen.

88-Year-Old Man Visits the Candy Shop

How many ways are there to dream
of heaven? Pearly gates? Passe,
some say—besides, oysters are sick
to death from man's tampering.
Streets of gold? A prey to fluctuations
of the market, and a temptation

to stray from narrow, base-metal ways.
The Dodge Caravan sat, ticking
its heat away, in the parking lot
of the Candy Store on Georgesville Rd.
The driver was inside, doing
Swisher Sweets, rounds of Maker's Mark

and Stroh's, screwing up courage
to buy a lap dance, maybe two.
He'd stopped on this pilgrim's progress
from undertaker to cemetery,
Wooster to Proctorville, spooked
by what he saw in the mirror,

to sneak a little peek at paradise,
leaving his passenger in the van
doing his best to be good,
eternity just three days old.
The day manager, Jolene (she
refused to give a last name,

out of modesty) expressed surprise
when told there was a corpse
outside. *Say, what kind of place
you think I run?* she said
with just a little fire, to the deputy
looking somewhere below

her chin. *My face is up here,
Buddy. I've seen the candy here
work miracles. A lap or table dance
can be just what the doctor ordered
to lift a man. But there's nothing
we can do for poor dear John out there,*

*so cold there's no fire hot enough.
We've got angel work enough inside.
The stiff will get his private room
all right, and no plain-clothes dicks
will try to sneak a peek inside.
He's on his back until the trumpet blows.*

Gunman Destroys the World Again

Today, because God told him to,
a Jordanian soldier opened fire
on seventh-grade Jewish girls

on a picnic outing to an island
in the Jordan River, killing seven,
wounding several, though, as

commentators were quick to say,
It Could Have Been Worse, the shooter
taking his stance, automatic fire,

fifty girls running down a hill,
screaming, slipping. I think about
my youth. Holding a Gibson Jumbo,

I played at protest, a '60s singer angry
about racism, carpet bombing, incursions
into Cambodia. I and a young woman

made a vow, *We won't bring children into
a world this bloody*. We kept the promise
all of two years. Three lives we've summoned

to a world no better—worse, I believe—
than the one we disdained with new eyes.
Our children will inherit a land

the gunman occupies, the old rage
behind his eyes. Crouching,
changing clips, he fires at little girls

who flee, desperate to escape
the dark tyranny of the news.
They run toward us. We stand

with open arms. We know the voices.
Daddy! Mommy! they cry.
It sounds like an accusation.

25 Hurt in Tent Collapse

A time for revival. 300 people. A tent,
60 feet by 100, out in the middle
of a beanfield, sudden thudding
of thunder. Wiffs of brimstone.

They shouted, yessed, stomped—
not like olden times, maybe,
but loud enough to kick the devil
in the ass. The winds, aroused,

licked madly under the flaps.
When ushers tried to close out
the whirlwind, the New Zion rose
in Ohio, then came down hard

and they were gone, sisters,
brethren, kids. Squads from Botkins,
Anna, Jackson Center, St. Johns
and Wapakoneta came wailing.

They drove first to the church,
expecting the usual apocalypse—
sewer gas, propane, bruises of ruin,
cracked brick, plumbing splayed,

crosses gone awry in the sky—
but no sign. Doors banged open,
closed, pews shiny, deserted.
They couldn't find a soul.

Clothed in their shiny gear,
vestments of catastrophe,
looking around, amazed, they
went out to look for bodies.

PART TWO

Pompeii in Danger

"I See a Dark Stranger in Your Future"

Rome's mayor wants to ban Gypsy fortune tellers.
    There's nothing
        picturesque about these people.
Is it good for tourists to be cursed
    if they refuse to have their palms read?

The mayor, incensed, addresses the scribbling press.
    The future insists,
        imposes itself on us,
importuning like an angry panhandler
    as we try to hide in the present. We refuse

to make eye contact. If we could,
    we'd cross the street
        to avoid tomorrow.
At the Trevi fountain, wishing stones
    erode from fumes of cabs, busloads

of Gap, Nikon, Gucci gawkers.
    At the Villa D'Este,
        fierce gargoyles
puke into cool reflecting pools.
    At Pompeii, writhing victims dance,

arms and palms upraised, as bright ash
    falls from heaven.
        Even at the Vatican,
the echoes of broken blessings drone
    down on us from a distant window.

Pompeii in Danger

—Reuters

Tourists, petty thieves,
graffiti
                    diddlers,
the weather
          of southern Italy—
the current peril, not
moody, fuming Vesuvius.
In 1956
64 Roman homes
     open to the public.
Today, but 14.
Last year,
     two million sweating visitors.
They pry up
mosaics.
         Fondle
         frescoes.   *Pompeii Red*
dulls to flat pink.
Where art
          is concerned
(not to mention
reality)
     people are
the problem.
         Cemetery doll houses.
Grave petting zoo.
Romans
       writhe,
contort in plaster.
        Living couples
come to touch,
             to screw,

imagining tons

of ash
                             falling
                             on their backs
like snow, muffled moans,
     the night
     a mountain
coming down.

The Road beneath the Road

Workers stumble on an old road
under Pisa's tower, leaning with
millennial seriousness of purpose.

In restauro and *Chiuso*, signs
read, *Under restoration* and *Closed.*
The tower is not to be put aright;

just stopped from crashing to
this Pisan earth, where once the sea
roared. We tourists need a guide

to show us towers leaning under
the ones looming above us,
basilicas, baptisteries, campaniles

filled with stony subterranean chant,
cool Blue Grottoes lapping
under the luminous caves

the boats of our shadow days
move through, busts strewn
under the feet of the statues

which gaze with egg-white eyes
on us, *villa* and *palazzo*
magnificent in opulent dark.

Tuscan cypress, twirled pines
of Rome, stately avenues run
beneath those which take us here

and there through the clutter
of our days, as we go the way
our parents went in their haste

to make of earth and stone a name,
a place, then slip beneath the grass
to walk away from us forever.

The Farm beneath the Farm

Every city rises over
    sites that used to be,
every fire. A boy, a girl
    stand over mother, father.

In southern Sicily, a farm
    five centuries old
found under a field
    farmed by an elderly couple.

Archaeologists from Siracusa
    discovered coins the dead
held in their ragged purses,
    grasping, bony hands,

a grindstone for milling
    the corn of hell,
semolina and farina
    out of the dirt of eternity,

clay basins for washing
    dust of centuries from
black, shriveling visages,
    shards of amphorae and plate

which these old farmers
    of the lower world set
on the table to celebrate
    their dark, timeless feasts.

Beneath every farm is another
    where ravenous beasts
root and chew, where nothing
    grows, everything grows.

Parish Priest Struck by Easter Bell

It bore the tone of legend—
                a body you'd known every day
suddenly not there when you
    most expect to watch it move
between candle flame and you.

The people of Forca di Valle
                called police when old Father Carmine
failed to show for Mass
    his biggest day, the rolling back
of the stone, the grand *Ta-Da!*

a body moving from nowhere
                to Sunday. Someone, remembering
how light the old can get,
    thought to look up, and then
they all recalled the bell that dawn.

It had been particularly clear,
                Like honey, they'd say later.
The last sound is the sweetest.
    He was found in the campanile,
a red pool beneath the head,

rope clutched in hand,
                and the doves, witnesses
to one of those mortal cries
    later sung as operatic miracle,
a dirty, mourning chorus.

Venice Declares War on Pigeons

—AP

for Dominic

There are photos and slides in a closet,
stored too in the dark of my skull.
A son of mine, still a child—though yesterday
I met the woman he says he'll marry—

stoops in the Piazza San Marco as if
he bore the weight of the ten pigeons who,
having achieved flight, surpassing
the bipedal waddle we do, having

dominion over their heavier brethren,
rise to claim his bag of popcorn.
His face is radiant, the moment of perfection.
(Is it only in childhood the soul

has such control over bone?)
It's as if by coming all the way
from Ohio to this magic place he holds
the scene together, even San Marco,

staggering Frankenstein monster
of beauty. My boy rises off stones to do
a little dance with lilting creatures,
birds which still today inhabit

the kingdoms of paper and air.
City authorities, citing disease, filth,
are bringing in nets, cylinders
of poison, army marksmen.

Amid the jewels, hourless breaths
of Byzantine gold, under the Campanile,
next to the Doges' Palace, a city
where death, water and light conspire

to elevate us, there is soon to be
a slaughter. I will find those photos,
carry them outside, start a fire. Smoke
from my pyre will twist off the paper.

Fat, dirty little angels will dance forever
on the shoulders of my smiling boy.

Funding the Dead

> *The Italian government has been paying disability pensions*
> *to 30,000 dead people, according to reports.*
> —Reuters

A country better than Egypt or China even
at paying homage to the ancestors.
The ultimate welfare state, reaching
beyond the grave. But what do the dead

need? Shelter? Taken care of. Loam
of Mother Earth, little stone manses,
cloud castles, urns and urns of pure ash.
No use for fettuccine, polenta, risotto,

Frescati, Chianti Classico, at least until
the tongue's resurrection, though
in *Italia* nothing is certain when it comes
to food. Sweaters and blankets for life

up there among pearlescent cumuli,
austere as the Alps? Buffeted
by prevailing winds, a soul learns
in a hurry to cover up. No need

for deodorant, body splash,
patchouli, Brute. The damned need
fan, air conditioner, *gelato limone,*
ice bucket. But how do the dead

cash their checks? Where in paradise
are the late-night carryouts?
How many pieces of ID do
the banks of hell require? In truth,

the news is everywhere in Italy
of ranks of corpses bearing
bogus disability papers, family favors
from corrupt doctors, uncles.

A full-time job—respectable, nearly—
playing dead in this sunny land
of ancient shade, goddesses galore,
legions of demons grinning forever

in repose while Carrara marble crumbles,
frantic arias of every day loud enough
to shake the catacombs, gold plains
of ruin, and wake the underworld.

Writing to the Holy Child of Aracoeli, Miracle-Maker

Each day the letters pile up at the shrine, a thick altar cloth of snow. *O Bambino Santo, my son is on crack, in a gang, his nose an open sore.* The monk who carved the child from Gethsemane wood was too poor to buy paint. Praying hard for color, *Caro Bambino, my jewel, only fifteen, has failed her PAP smear again because a bad boy puts his thing in her when I'm at work and there is no father at home to put the fear into them* he fell asleep, and in his dream an angel came to paint the statue with its flaming wings, the air a flurry of crayons. A storm *O Baby-god, a rouged little girl, stockinged, lipsticked, high-heeled, struts on stage swinging what are not yet a woman's hips, legs hairless* swamped the boat bringing the Bambino to Italy. The frantic passengers tossed overboard *before the sharp pencils of the judges, and now this baby girl is dead in the very dead of night, garroted, head bashed in, a cord* everything, including the Child, to lighten things. Three days later He bobbed into Livorno's harbor, *wrapped around her cold, pretty, unpulsing throat. The police haven't a clue. The first officer on the scene bonded with the mother and neglected to secure the crime scene. The so-called ransom note is a bad joke. The prosecutors are having coffee, golfing with the defense team. O Child of the World, we chase and chase them through the rooms, stomping like thunder,* kick wet and tired but smiling. The church of Santa Maria in Aracoeli on the Campidoglio marks the shrine *our children in the stomach for wetting the bed, for crying, for not saying Yes Sir, extinguish cigarettes on their cheeks, force their fingers into the pot of scalding Campbell's Chicken Noodle Soup, onto the very ring of blue kitchen fire, visit their quaking beds like an awful dream, thrust sharp, blunt objects into them, the ribs of our precious angels a latticework of hurt, the worst we can do, all because they must we must be taught a lesson, because we can, and so we write these sad letters to heaven which fall back to earth like so much dirty snow.*

The Land of Liars

A survey of Italians said 70% had confessed to telling between five and ten lies every day.
—Reuters

In the land of Pinocchio, where even wood can come to life at a magic word or two, up and down both coasts, from the Alps to Milan, Pisa to Bologna to Venice and Rome, even in Assisi, especially at the Vatican, around Naples, throughout Calabria and Sicily of course, noses are growing. Two-thirds are women who lie in love. *There was never anyone but you. He wasn't the man you are. None of the others meant a thing to me. My God you are so big you are killing me. O Christ! O Jesus! Of course I did. How can you ask that? It's never been that good before. I've never said those words before.* Men are more likely to lie on the job. *Not a problem. It's been taken care of. Yes I know all about that. It's in the mail. It's not my fault. That's not my responsibility. But I told you about it. I told him just what you told me. You never told me that. She was begging me for it.* 27% lie to cover up errors. *God, if you grant me this I'll never ask another favor. I'll go to church every day. I'll stop doing . . . you know what.* 42% lie to avoid conflict. *How nice to see you. I haven't told a soul. Of course I've forgiven you. I'll miss you more than I can say.* 21% lie for the good of someone else. *This is better than my mother makes it. Actually I prefer my pasta limp and soft, my wine sweet as candy. That looks great on you. I was just thinking about you. I swear on my mother's grave. I can't live without you. I'll never lie to you. I've never lied to you before. I have lied to you before but this is the gospel truth. Everything I've said is true, essentially.*

Il Giorno to Close

—Reuters

The Milan paper, bleeding more
than two trillion lire a year, is to
shut down. After today, due to
lack of capital, not to mention interest,
there will be no more of the day.

No more light-time enlightenment.
In Italy too, news fades too soon,
local concerns drowning
in Southern disaster, national crisis.
Tomorrow, readers of *Il Giorno*

must be content with later—
Corriere de la Sera, perhaps,
Evening Courier. A tree falls
in the far forest to be squeezed
and rolled into what was.

What do we do when the day
grows too dear? How we ache
to be told everything we've lost.
The light fails, to be spread
at evening's feet, then crumpled,

to skitter down windy streets,
gather in darkening corners,
dry whispers, and then, a thump
at the door to announce
the arrival of *La Notte*, the night.

Doctors in Italy Transplant Heart of a Baby Born without a Brain

—Reuters

Another miracle. The sort
of medical news we're inured to,
nearly. Bambina Gabriella, born
in Turin without cranium or brain

but breathing without aid, gave
her heart to Bambino Maurizio,
born the same day in Rome
at Bambino Gesu Hospital,

bearing a broken heart. The Pope
wrote his congratulations
to Gabriella's parents, thanking them
for courageously accepting God's plans.

*O darling girl, mindless one, who's
to say you're not the luckiest?
You could breathe and feel yet
never grow to days too cloudy*

*for signs, a world that always
has been brutal to innocents.
Your tiny heart beats on.
Such love you gave.* No brain,

holes in a heart—a bad day
for God, though some would say
it's all part of a master plan.
Babies gasp, writhe and expire,

pink and blue bundles, little puddles
of fate. What never dies, given
our situation, cradle to grave,
is the need for miracles.

Nonna, Who, the Last 50 Years, Burned a Candle Every Day

Thick lips, never satisfied. Big ears
hear too much. Small hands can't
get it done. You have all three,
you're done for. American bread?

Tasteless. Soft. Like American church.
Good priest? Bad prostate.
You can't tell if a girl is beautiful
until she's old. *If looks could kill,*

they say here. In Calabria they do
every day. Only three redheads
in the history of history were faithful:
the Holy Calf of Sorrento

(who warmed the Bambino with
his breath in snowy Bethlehem),
Mary Magdalene, and then
you have Jesus. She and He

got married at Cana, because,
well, they had to. Nice wedding.
The food could have fed all
Cleveland for a year.

There was much drinking.
The wine ran out. They needed
a miracle. Christ had a mother.
I don't need to tell the rest.

Virgin Cries Tears of Olive Oil

The papier-mache Virgin
had been weeping for months,
lips and breasts sloppy
with the lusts of the world,
the crisp efficiency of the rich,
their new money. Thousands
of pilgrims made the arduous way
to the village deep in the South
to weep with her. The statues
of Rome and Naples may bleed
like high-C tenors, grandly;
like pro wrestlers, with flair;
but tiny tears are good enough
for Puglia. The priest—dreams
of a lifetime realized, so many years
in this village of puny plots,
stunted trees—was proud
Our Lady chose his church
as the provincial stage,
an out-of-the-way dark where
she could perform, and help
his career. But the bishop wasn't sure.
He had a sample sent to the lab
in Catanzaro. *A substance
very like olive oil, with
no biological human trace,*
the report came back.
The Men of the Church,
somber in black, flamboyant
in stoles and robes, say "Fake."

Certainly. And yet, any mother
in a land of hard earth can cry
tears of salt. To weep pure oil
of olive *extra vergine*—drops of light,
savor, fire—is a miracle worthy
of a goddess, a people
poor as stone and needing
to believe there is a place
where everything is of more use
than what they're given here,
even the tears.

The Death of Domenico Modugno

The newspaper claims that so popular over the decades has your "Volare" grown some want to make it the new Italian national anthem. And why not? Still it seems to me the day things Italian-American came out of the closet and owned up, too far beneath the *Quattrocento* to be calculated of course but still miles higher than bathtub shrines of painted Madonnas holding pudgy *Bambino* cupids, male fantasies of heavenly mothers, perfect sluts. Still it plays in the darkening room where my memories are stacked teetering against the walls nearly to the spider-webbed ceiling, and the old turntable wobbles and spins. *Volare. Wo-o. Cantare. Wo-o-o-o. Fly. Sing.* To do one was to practice the other, I believed. Lyrics inspired by figures navigating Chagall's azure and mystical heaven, the obituary goes on to say, star-eyed peasant lovers and mules afloat above the *shtetls* soon to be drowned out by the thunder of panzers, click of cyanide pellets, bitter smoke of the great ovens. *We can leave the confusion and all disillusion behind.* Fields like those of your native Puglia (though for years, a deputy in parliament and champion of the disabled but unable to accept your crippled self, you pretended to be mysterious, a Sicilian Gypsy), a memory from some distant world receding down lanes twisting to the village and away. *Nel blu dipinto di blu*, the actual title, *In Blue Painted Blue*, but today we remember only the soaring chorus. *Vo-la-re.* What did I learn from you? That flying alone is dangerous, and thus we must try together. The sin of Icarus, after all, is that he forgot his father and filled heaven with the sun. *Just like birds of a feather, a rainbow together we'll find. Volare. Wo-o. Cantare. Wo-o-o-o.* Birds, archangels and all the communion of saints learn to confound gravity and time, to grow light and full of song enough to lift into the profound, pristine blue, to make their great escape. And now, I read and understand, you.

PART THREE

The Penmanship of the Dead

Thoreau's Site Fouled by Nature

Walden experience turns malodorous
—AP

I met Poe at St. Ignatius High School,
third period, after geometry and before Caesar.
The rank miasma of the tarn bubbled
over Roderick Usher one morning
as I rode the Rapid Transit from
the white side of the city over the slow river
of petrochemicals on my way to early Mass.
How he loved his sister, who suddenly
had gone away. He hurt her beyond words.
The things he heard in that horrible house.
Evil grew, a mildew on the walls, his brain.
On the other hand, Henry David's cabin
was clean. I imagined his starched collar,
face scrubbed with Walden water, armies
of ants battling at his feet, though he stayed
ever above the fray. He would think,
then sweep some more. Whatever lasts
long enough gets dirty. The stink is thought
to be coming from bacteria rotting
in the sand. Swimmers who thrilled
to slip beneath the Walden surface, believing
they were being cleansed in the essence
of America, must travel now to town
to the municipal pool, freshly painted,
chlorinated, clean in the modern sense.
We never thought nature was capable
of turning us away. We don't belong,
Walden is whispering. Thoreau himself
was occupier, squatter. And though
we saw it sink beneath the waters of the tarn,
that dark, foreboding house is still here.
We're inside, frantic at the bolted door.

Making Time

In *Durée et simultanéité,* Bergson tells us
there's proper clock time and time
the cartoon way we humans do it, snowball
rolling down slope, fast yielding to faster,

eddied rush of stream. It took me forever
to read the book. The neighbor's dog,
no longer yipping as it did the summer before
when it was a pup, kept a deeper rhythm.

Reading a book in French on the nature
of time, I was Sisyphus. My mind
would wander to the way a certain woman
puts on her makeup while watching me

on the bed in the mirror watching her
line and daub, painstaking attention to hue
and shade. She was teaching me the suspense
of passion, the time it takes her to put on

stockings. Quick as summer storm, we take
the stockings off. Later, I recall this while
I should be reading, the heart going slow,
fast, seizing the moment, using it up.

The Death of a Friend Who Still Believes

—for Big Ed

One day a friend calls to say
    another friend is dead, news
you can't use, a body
    sprawled in the bathroom
at dawn, the sudden hurt
    about your own heart

as you summon up a face,
    the fat Irish laugh—and
just like that a life closes
    with the customary *Hello*.
One day a friend, perhaps
    this same messenger,

will make a call to say
    it's *you* who won't be
turning up at lunch forever.
    There was a time even news
this bad was acceptable,
    God in His heaven,

Jesus an old-time operator
    connecting you to Central,
Maker and Taker. The deceased
    believed in God, and I
was one among our group
    who teased his stolid credence,

calling him pie-eyed, drunk
    on cheap-wine wonder. He
lived for happy endings, grace
    and redemption rendered
in slabs, pats, butter melting
    on toast, thick gravy ladled

on the roast, the mutt left behind
    walking hundreds of miles
to rejoin the family, the kids
    giggling with joy. I pray—
and this of course is just
    a phrase I use, no more—

he didn't change his mind,
    cold stroke of *Oh no, no*
seizing him the last moment.
    I hope it was Jesus
he thought he'd gotten
    on the line, not nothing

at all, or a wrong number.
    I hope he felt to the end
that this was the prize
    chosen just for him,
the big one, the call he'd
    longed for all his life.

The Desertion of the Frogs

1.
U.S. Keds left on the bank, jeans
rolled, we waded the creek, scooped
the polliwogs into the Miracle Whip jar.

With the holes punched in the lid
with Father's awl, we thought we knew
the future. We came home, stood

dumb as ox, ass and We Three Kings
at the manger, horny for miracle.
Our prey looked scary up close,

sperm bloated by rays from Planet X.
Their eyes kept saying *How could you?*
A discovery of ignorance and magic.

We thought they'd grow to bullfrogs
big as puppies, to croak the garage
all summer long. They only died,

floated to the top, tails still, eyes
like blisters. So many times I've killed.
This may have been the first.

2.
She kissed the tall, hunky prince,
gave him tongue, some T and A,
a whole lot more. He shrank

into a loathsome toad and fled.
Her lips were studded warts,
and that damp place between

her legs. Her tongue bulged,
a fat gherkin. She drank a teacup
of battery acid. A man in tights,

a cape and crown ran in the door,
flesh burning, kneeling, asking,
between screams, for her hand.

She hopped away. Now, sick
of our never-ending Once-upon-
a-times, the frogs are leaping

from our lives. No more miracles.
Gone, from every night's pond,
the grunts, the grand croaks of love.

Tools

The shepherd, watering his flock
at the muddy, dying lake, deep
in the season of East African drought,

saw them too late, eyes tiny, nostrils
big with thirst at the stink of water,
their way blocked by bleating sheep.

A staff and crook are little defense.
Who knows which chimpanzee picked up
the first one. *He that is without sin,*

let him first cast a stone, the monkey savior
might have preached, had he not
been eaten long ago. The shepherd

went down hard under the stunning hail,
prey to the needs of beasts, a heap of bones
broken and numbered. Even the apes

have mastered tools, stripped branch
thrust down tunnel or hole to capture
a mouthful of termites or ants, tickle

and burn of bitter, sweet or salt, or stone
to crush beetle, nut or skull. I recall a day
my friends and I defended the creek bank

from a tribe of boys we didn't know.
They were coming to plash at us, force us
to flee, when I found a scattered cache

of sweetly stinking crabapples littering
the ground. We had the means to send
the strangers back where they came.

The sky, and then the creek, full of apples,
the invaders vanquished, the odor
and stain of victory on our fists.

For ages, we've been guilty of tools, swollen
with what we can do with a good idea
in our hands. We think they absolve us.

I didn't do it. It was the victim. It was
this burning thirst, shape of the obsidian knife,
the apple, stone, fitting my hand perfectly.

Payday

Whiskey river take my mind, Willy sings.
And it has. In the mirror of the room
of the Star Bar that reads *Gents,*
stink of Marlboros, Swisher Sweets, piss.

I grin at myself with eyes that, when
they focus, look foolish. Who's grin is this,
shit eatin', teeth peeking though numb lips?
The guys back at my table, laborers

from Tennessee and West Virginia,
whose workbenches are next to my own
48 hours a week, goaded me—a teenager
doing shots and beers—until I asked

the pretty girl sitting alone at a table
to dance. *Sure,* she said, swinging back
her long braid, pretty eyes cast low.
We danced until he cut in. *Keep*

your goddamn hands off my wife,
the cinder-block wall of a man, biceps
like fat hams, said loud enough
for the whole place to hear over

David Houston's *Almost Persuaded.*
Last night, all alone in a barroom, met
a girl with a drink in her hand. He
could have taken out every tooth, but

the humiliation was punishment enough,
he knew. The guys at my table laughed
hard as I returned, a dumbass kid
who'd let his guard down, breathing fast,

cheeks hot, a hard lesson from a man
who knows what real work means.
Sometimes the fights you don't have
are the ones you lose the worst. Now,

reeling, I grip the sink to steady myself.
Straight white teeth peek out at me
from the mirror. A young man
with a future privileged and grand.

Naming a Wildflower, a Mountain, a Night

Wild carrot or *Queen Anne's lace.*
Given choice between native and colonial,
how will we say the filigreed wildflower

strewn along blurs of July highway
near ice-blue *chicory* (or *Cichorium intybus?*)
Alaskans have changed the mountain back

to *Denali, The Big One*—the sacred name
the Athabaskan folk shouted in prayer—
from *McKinley*, coined by a white prospector

in 1896 to lift a dull Republican candidate.
David, I became in Cleveland in 1947,
along with a peasant cognomen, to replace

the utter nothing I was, when, to put
a spell on a cold night, tongues dancing,
they said one another, a woman and a man.

Nomen Est Omen:
A Name Is Destiny

I say that nothing is more important than names.
—Whitman

The year I went from high school *Dave*
to college *David*, I blamed it on love. She
would sing it as we lay in woods and fields
of Southern Ohio, sheets of the Acropolis Motel
across the border in Parkersburg,

along with *O my God.* Sweet christening.
Many of those referred by the courts
for psychiatric evaluation have names
that make their days a wound,
Oder, Lethal, Iago, Adolf, God.

Because we were nearly children ourselves,
our first (can it be?) was nearly *Greer*—
a baby named for a star. *Uhura,* the woman
in the supermarket said when I asked
what I should call her babe—

she wouldn't use for this flawless jewel
the nomenclature of another race
or a word that said *Slave.* This is
the way we utter one another.
A name, a wish, a curse, a prayer.

The Meeting

So often these days
I find myself sitting
in the wrong meeting.

The procession of words
jerks, plods its way around
the lovely table, wood

dark as my father's eyes
when, as a child, I displeased
him, or the confessional

I rode, those days, over flames
of everlasting hell,
or the rude, varnished cross

worn smooth with centuries
of wet, immodest kisses.
The speakers hold to the agenda

the way the dying clutch
their wills. The words
are tired birds circling.

The speakers are smart.
They know the numbers,
and their shoes are glossed

to a terrible importance,
while mine, scruffy and sad,
tell the world I do not

mean business. *Fellow*
members of the committee,
I move we adjourn forever,

*walk out to find the graves
of our parents, kneel, pull
weeds away from their names,*

*ask ourselves what we're making
of these precious seconds.
O Mother, Father, if*

*there were more people
like me in this world,
nothing would get done.*

Hound Dog

Having adjusted ringlets of hair, pretty flax anklet, worked the needle into my arm, started the IV, fretting over, petting me long enough to assure herself it has begun—the three-hour drip, afternoon sun falling into my arm, filling my mouth with lead—the nurse leaves. I'm chained here for the duration, a diver at the end of my rope, cosmonaut trying to keep *Mir* from crumbling around me (but I realize *Mir* is my own obsolete body), the BP guy in greasy coveralls pumping prehistory's precious essences back up to the wreck of the present. Let there be music, time a body can hear. Which CD will it be? Aida, strident urgencies of an Ethiopian slave girl caught in the chains of empire, her lover Radames cursed by Isis and the mincing, blaring priests of Egypt? Entombment forever and ever Amen? Opera always brings out the melodramatic worst in me. Not today. Let's make it something more true than the grand stage, the sort of thing a lover says when things are going all to hell. Here's Big Mama Thornton, carrying her "Ball & Chain," which Joplin tried so hard to drag around, and now she's scolding, scalding the real Hound Dog, a tune not even the Jordanaires could save for Elvis, who, for all the gyrations—dry humping more frantic than high school Friday nights—still came across as wooden, tied to his guitar, too damn white. I'm on a leash. *You ain't nothin' but a hound dog, been snoopin' round the door.* Sing it, Big Mama Time. Give it to me. I deserve it, every note.

Spiders, Worms, the History of MS

In the lab, worms learn blind alleys
of the maze by eating worms
who've learned the hard way.

Spiders fed the hot blood of
a schizophrenic weave wild webs,
intemperate cities they get lost inside.

The portrait of my MRI brain
glows like the moon, a brilliance
that illuminates the room, but 24 lesions,

holes bright as nothing, give me
a new name. How will it read,
the web of the spider spinning

through my skull? Brother Worm,
will I make you shrivel, writhe?
We are what we leave behind,

the hungers we inspire.

Two Lessons from the Sky

1. Africa

Sometimes I think too much about the devolution of a
body, the word *sclerosis* becoming more difficult to say,
my legs jerking to some music of their own, eyes oblivious
to beauty's necessary specifics. I long to be as light as
the African moth, *Lobocraspis greisifusa*, which lives on
nothing but the tears of elephants, fluttering up to sip
salt nectar from sad eyes which look down on a minuscule,
blurred world.

2. Ohio

And the birds at Hueston Woods roosting in the beech
and sugar maples ringing Lake Acton—birds I thought,
through heavy, prismatic plastic, were red-tailed hawks.
They proved even lovelier when, afloat on six-foot span
of grandiloquent wings strong enough to spin this heavy
world and lift it close enough to taste, eyes so keen they
can seek out and unearth the tiniest bit of lifelessness, dark
blossoms of Ohio acres below, so easy in their gravity,
soaring above where we were walking, they came close
enough to tell me that the lightness I want is even now on
the wing, to whisper the truth: *Turkey vulture.*

Reading the MRI Report, the Retired Pastor Considers Dementia

Days when the body tells me it's found
another way to say *Oh no you don't*,
I try not to think about the nothing
I'll become—except perhaps in the minds
of those who know me, the hearts
of the few who love—when I go to ash.

(Not that I'll be able actually to *do* anything
about it. The ash I mean.) *Stop thinking*,
I say to myself, as you'd say to a child
No talking in church. I've two ways
of talking to myself inwardly (*inwordly*,
I almost wrote), my intimate monologue.

There's the way I say using words,
as if I were speaking *on the record*
for someone listening in on my thoughts.
(This may come from a noisy childhood,
my head filled with garrulous saints,
angels, demons, and the three Gods,

one of whom—or is it Whom?—had wings
and cooed like a bird.) Then there is
the lightning, too-fast-to-hear thought
by which I will myself to jerk the car
from chattering squirrels or kids going
from one oak or game to another

across the road, the wordless ways
I communicate with mind, heart, arm.
Don't give it another thought, the saying goes.
How can I (not)? I can't know I'm not
thinking. No voices. No chants. Nothing—
but keeping track of the nothing is now

the postmodern occupation, itself
a thought, perhaps the most important one
we have. No way out of this haunted church
of neurons. We scream at ourselves,
or whisper, or make that silent speech
inside the confessional of dark old bone.

Is the voice I use when I talk to myself
as much like Mother's and Father's as
my outside voice? His (capital here
because he begins a sentence, not
as a theological statement) was always
too loud, especially when I was near,

though still he can shout great distances.
Ten states over. I don't know how
Mother sounds inside her head, for all
our love. No one yet—for real—has heard
the inner voice of another, though many
lovers claim they know the foreign accents

of God. (What does His—some now add
or Hers) sound like to the angels?
To Himself (Herself)? Can all three cast-
members of the Trinity speak at once?
While I'm losing the knowledge necessary
to mouth words to myself, thinking

more slowly *Hey, listen, to me. I'm
thinking!* might I also be losing it
that other way, beyond mere words,
eluding, exceeding the drag of syllables,
a nighthawk dipping, diving above
ripe fields, earth rising quickly, stones.

Tabloid Poem

In the Big Bear Supermarket
at the very end of my street
are tiers and tiers of foodstuffs,
counters shining bright as televisions
with one hundred hams, rolls
of braunschweiger and bologna stacked
like munitions, ziggurats of Gala apples,
kiwi fruit, Bartlett pears, arugula,
radicchio. I want to believe
in the limitless bounty of this glistening West,
its vast lands running to the gold horizon.
I pick out cans, squat little peasants
labeled *Contadina*, sweetness picked
by brown-skinned migrants who journeyed
all the way to northwest Ohio to help me
make the sauces I learned
from my peasant Nonna, a *contadina*
herself, who grew and picked her own.
The cereal screams at me from lurid boxes!
Oh, sweet, sweet roughage, oats, fiber!
I make it to the pet aisle where animals
eat better than babies of the Third World.
I take refuge in the aisles of belief
where mortals leave their laden carts
with wheezing wheels and float
in realms of awful wonder. Now
I'm safe to dream, the *Housewife*
Who Lives in Hell, Scared to Death
of Germs, Bat-Boy on the Loose
at the Mall, Hunting Blood
of Plump Virgin Girls, Space-alien Dad
Up All Night Probing and Probing
the Neighbors, Hapless Traveler
Raped by Biker Dykes and Kept
as Sex Slave for Three Years.
I can't wait to tell you what they did to me.

The Thawing of the Iceman

In Bolzano, on a slab in a gleaming lab
    at the South Tyrol Museum of Archaeology
        the great Iceman of the Alps is thawing,
    traveling slowly back to soft, a state
he's not visited for 5,300 years,

when the avalanche took his light away.
    Like the moaning plant-man who fell
        from outer space in *The Thing*, and gave
    me nightmares in the '50s (though
to tell it true I felt sorry for him,

marooned on our cold, colorless world
    so far from a sun of any magnitude),
        he seeps, leaves a telltale puddle beneath,
    naughty little boy who'll cause a ruckus
soon enough. Scientists will take

their samples of bone, DNA,
    contents of his last meal. They'll snake
        an endoscope far up his intestines, scrape
    enamel from back molars to calculate
strontium and lead. We never learn.

Like sleeping dogs, aliens should be
    let alone to doze their days, keeping
        ours safe. As violins and theremin
    rise and fall, ice picks prick the spine.
Things are about to get scary.

My immune system is eating
    the myelin that sheathes nerve cells
        of spinal cord and brain. Now an alien
    to myself, *Sclerosis Man*, I slide out
of the sci-fi MRI to amaze the troupe

of white-coated medicos mapping
    my lesions. Cold as it is for me,
        things could be worse. What if,
    by science, pollution, mischance,
I'm pulled screaming from forever

like that Cold-War movie Thing?
    I reel and lurch. Sirens sweep
        the streets. Screaming mothers grab
    children as they run, the army
mobilizing, missiles bristling.

May he rest in peace. Do Not Resurrect.

A Brief History of Fathers

Do we miss a thing we love
less if, in going away from us,
it grows beautiful? It rained

all weekend, and the leaves
this morning are going
from brown and tan to crimson.

The splendor flaming from
these trees compensates us,
nearly, for what autumn takes

leaf by leaf, the lined white face
of a father growing noble
the angrier, more confused

he goes, rain like angry bees,
his empty eyes, a cold wind
coming on like dementia.

Calling Mother

Some boys stay boys, splashing in that milky rapture,
face of the goddess looming big as the moon.
I'd write each week, but needed to hear her voice.
Not only Italian sons. The paper says Israeli soldiers

on patrol are calling on cell phones. *Mom, they're
being mean as hell. Not just the enemy. I'm not eating
right.* Mommyism, this is called in the War College,
a national crisis, colonels drafting reports,

love hampering the war effort. What if David
had been able to phone Bethlehem before slung stone
found the coordinates of glory? Mothers can't abide
the thought of blood from any mother's son.

I forget, go to grasp receiver and dial, though it's been
nine months since she took my hand, eyes
tiny with morphine, heart faltering. *I want to die*,
she said. *It's time. You have been my shining star.*

Such flattery, even at the end. Always she knew
what made me tick. I told the doctors she wanted out.
*Hello. Mom, how are you getting on? Dad makes toast
all day long. I trim and trim his mustache, trying*

*to make ends even, but it's no use. In this world
everything ends up single, as you understood
at the end there strapped and tubed to that high bed.
Tell me the weather in your new country*

*is better even than Fort Myers, the rivers of paradise
serene and bright as the Caloosahatchee, angels
leaping like mullet, no sprawl of malls with flags
big as billboards, so the aged ones can find them.*

*Tell me, dear, there's no need for morphine, no pain
to sear the lips that melted the ice I held to them,
harsh incense of bread smoking in the toaster,
no lost child waking suddenly to remember, to mourn.*

Song of the Bone

Afloat on tides that lapped our saline womb,
I woke to rolling thunder, one huge heart.
Beyond the suck and splash, her scents washed doom
out of my ears. She cooed to me to start
eternity, a voice God-loud inside our room
of fetal sea. I've always been a part
of her, and now, though she is in her tomb,
she still can say my name, the wind's wild harp
that whistles through my bones, a loom
that weaves a coat of song to soothe the dark.
And still today I spend those jewels of spume
she breathed, the notes blown true, or flat, or sharp.
    I floated blind, and there she was, my shore;
    her gift was all of time, and nine months more.

The Penmanship of the Dead

Rummage through a life's closets
long enough, you'll unearth artifacts,
a family's flint implements, ash of old flame,
bones fragile as a terra-cotta saint,
a 1959 Topps Rocky Colavito smelling
of bubble gum, Christmas cards from Nonna
in her flourishing Old World script.

The other day I came upon a tape,
gift from a dear friend in the days
before CDs—talk about ancient!—
but the best love bides its time
for years until the light comes back.
I'd praised *Qui mi frena,* the sextette
from *Lucia di Lammermoor,*

and down in his basement bar
where he called himself *The Queen
of Opera,* while Mother, his goddess,
padded about in slippers upstairs,
he'd recorded tunes he thought
I'd like. There, inside the case,
the play list in his best school hand,

serpentine loop and whorl, vowels
like open mouths, T's crossed obliquely,
daring ascensions, awful falls,
the music of words. Reading, I'm
his audience again, as, large Scotch
in hand, he teaches me opera, notes
of passion crashing around us. *Au fond*

du temple, from *The Pearl Fishers.*
Verdi's soaring *Bella figlia del amore.*
"The world won't let me love my way,"
he cries. "It's Mother. The news
would destroy her." Rising violins.
A few years after she was taken,
I recited Whitman over a son's grave.

The music endures. And this script.
What did we lose when we decided
not to teach our children to write
with grace? Whatever did we think
mattered more than penmanship,
this lush swearing to the truth,
arduous dancing between the lines?

Today no one cares about making words
by hand, and serious singers are dying
in all the old ways or of this plague
erasing many of our finest names.
It's getting harder to remember, to read
one another, but every now and then,
if we're lucky, the music returns,

a love letter from the dead.

Sister Mary Appassionata on the Grand Unified Theory

The layers of creation—
zebra and wapiti, weasel,
tapeworm, deer tick, nouns
of all sorts, brick and steel,
the fine, distant diamonds
that dangle between Orion's legs
from his glittering belt, even
this hand coming out of the sleeve
of its habit to move chalk
across blackboard, scraping nails
across the slate from time to time
to wake the loser-snoozers—these
are fermions (quarks, anti-
quarks, mesons). And now I'm
writing the word *leptons*
(electrons, muons, taus, neutrinos),
the fine print of the contract
we've signed with matter.
These careen around the nucleus
like muscle cars of the senior boys
let out after last period,
their best girls (skirts sliding up,
cracking their gum) hanging
all over them. Bosons (photons,
gluons, W's and Z's) make
our days stick to one another
like the sweet belly-sweat of lovers
dancing. I'm sorry to report
we can't find the graviton
to save our lives, yet such
a good idea must have weight.
String theory—branes humming

in ten dimensions—explains
how creatures as irregular
as boys and girls can come together
to make an almost perfect fit.
But a theory of absolutely everything,
grand and unified, needs more,
someone to stand outside
to prove it true, watchers
who like to watch the watched.
In all the universe *we*
are the principals of uncertainty.
So there you have it, though
there is a place it all makes sense,
where stars align for every gazer
into the highest name
of every good, a cosmos
humming with love indivisible.
Let's rearrange our desks again
and see what we can see.

Cell Phone

This is the awful music of our days. A cell phone
rings and rings. We lift it to our ear, and all at once dust

falls over lower Manhattan and the Pentagon, and dust
blows all the way to Columbus, our state's name now

two moans around a shriek of grief, disbelief, *Oh!–Hi!-Oh!*,
dust darkening the Olentangy and Scioto, Alum Creek,

all rivers running down to the Ohio, up to Lake Erie,
caking our faces and hair, so that we are all the same hue,

black ones, brown, yellow, red and white suddenly ashen,
streaked with tears like those ancient ones who mourned

in dust and ash. Look at us. We're older than ever we've been.
Sirens rise, and those thunders we'll never forget,

louder than our laboring hearts. I know you're not going
to believe this, but buildings have disappeared! Now,

words unimaginable. *Hello, Honey. It's me. Your husband,
loving wife, your baby girl. I'm calling from far above, below.*

*It doesn't look good. I want you to know whatever happens
to me I love you. If you love me back, promise this never*

*will happen again to anyone. You'll hear my voice again
never, except in your mortal dreams, the troubled winds.*

You'll never be again as you were. Click. He's gone!
She's no longer there! Now what are we going to do?

O citizens, we must never forget how precious are
those voices who've gone out of our lives, those songs

the history of loss and regret. How easily they slip away,
breaths soft as snowfall, as innocent as the stars

ticking above. *Mom. Can you hear me? Dad? Squeeze
my hand if you're still with us.* We must calculate

the distance between the worst and best we can be.
We've been burned by the fires scouring vast craters

of hatred, barred cells of closed minds. And we've seen
a gathering spirit deep and inexhaustible, a hospice

of hands reaching out to hands that need, the toiling
of rugged archangels in uniform, helmets, thick coats.

When do they sleep, we wonder? A phone rings.
All over the world, the phones go off. *Hello. I love you.*

*I'm on a plane. I'm sitting at my desk, looking
at your picture, our sweet babies. It doesn't look good.*

*There's three of us who are going to do something
about it. Let's roll. Goodbye. Hello. I love you. Goodbye.*

Hello, Mommy! The building is on fire. I can't breathe.
The messages continue, murmurs and words

from beyond the stink of this smoldering world.
They're trying to reach us, knowing we're running

out of time. *Find a way,* they say, *to persevere,
if not to love, at least to live with one another.*

*After injustice is punished, realize you are one
and the same, whatever your fictions of difference.*

*As terrible as you feel now, our going must give hope,
show how desperate a life can be when you forget*

*what being human means. Accept this life that is
your gift. Learn your way out of the tunnels of dark*

*to the beauty inside that makes us worthy of each other.
Goodbye. Hello. Goodbye. Hello. Goodbye. Hello.*

About the Author

David Citino is the author of twelve volumes of poetry, including the National Book Critics Circle Notable Book, *Broken Symmetry*. He is the contributing editor of *The Eye of the Poet: Six Views of the Art and Craft of Poetry*. His poems have appeared in numerous publications and anthologies, including *The Georgia Review, Kenyon Review, The Southern Review,* and *Threepenny Review*. Citino is professor of English and creative writing at The Ohio State University. He also serves on the Board of Trustees of the Greater Columbus Arts Council and of Thurber House and as poetry editor at the Ohio State University Press.

www.ingramcontent.com/pod-product-compliance
Lightning Source LLC
Chambersburg PA
CBHW021913180426
43198CB00034B/405